CULTIVATING GOD'S EARTH WITH VERSE

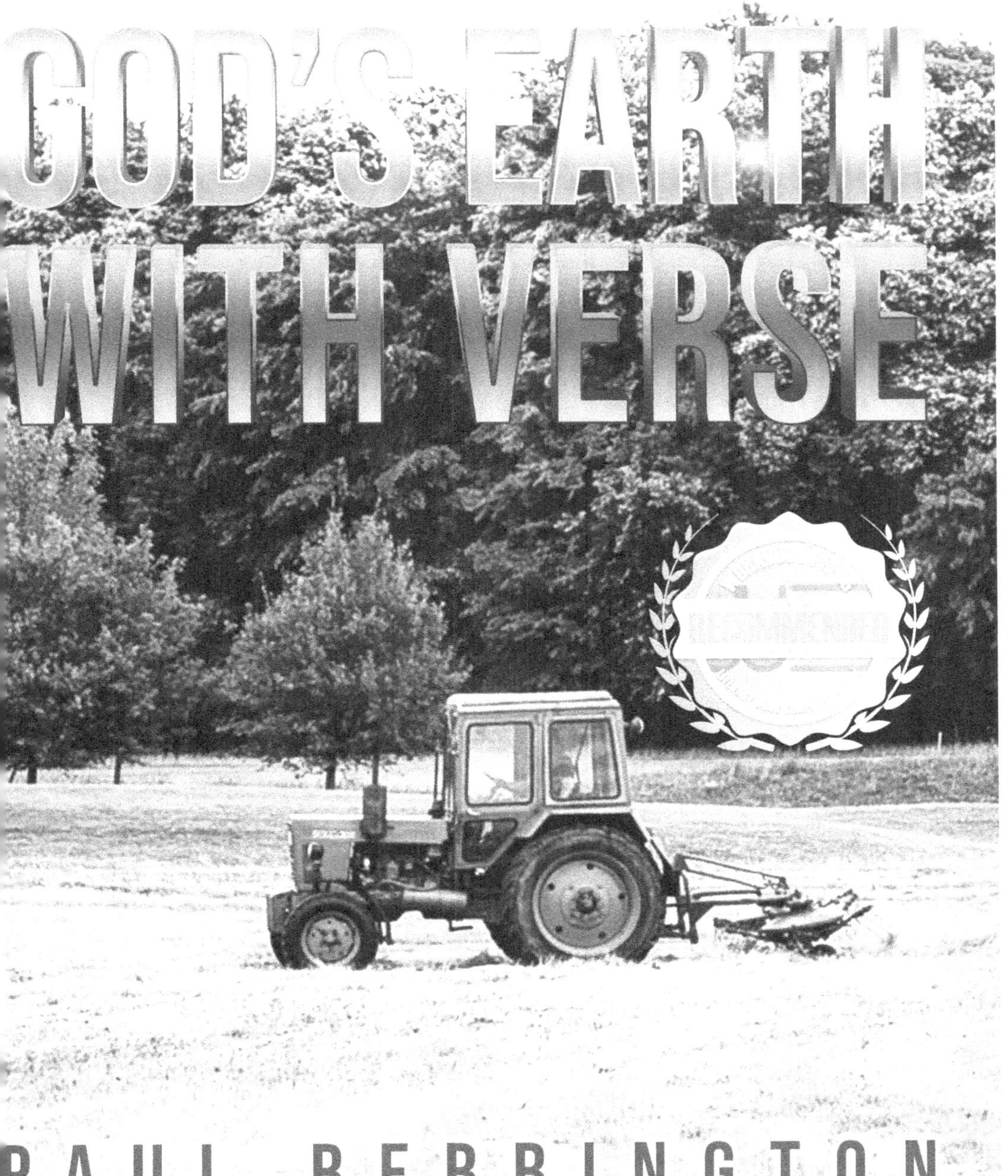

PAUL BEBBINGTON

WORKBOOK PRESS LLC
187 E Warm Springs Rd,
Suite B285, Las Vegas, NV 89119, USA

Website: https://workbookpress.com/
Hotline: 1-888-818-4856
Email: admin@workbookpress.com

Ordering Information:
Quantity sales. Special discounts are available on quantity purchases by corporations, associations, and others.
For details, contact the publisher at the address above.

Library of Congress Control Number:
ISBN-13:   978-1-956876-59-8 (Paperback Version)
                978-1-956876-60-4 (Digital Version)

REV. DATE: 01/12/2021

CULTIVATING GOD'S EARTH WITH VERSE

The Face2Face Educational Trust, is operated by Kevin Moore.

Kevin Moore uses art and chess in creative ways with people aged 6 to 80 years old. He operates from the Art Centre in the Charles Burrell Centre, Thetford.

He facilitates the annual Sketchpad holiday, for young people from 9 to 17 years old. He also speaks and leads services in East Anglia, and heads outreach events especially to children , to proclaim the Christian message.

Kevin also runs the Thetford Chess Club each week. He is married to Val, a nurse, and together they have 3 grown up children.

Admiral Alights

Excitement rose from that dense wood
As climbing o'er the fallen oak
I saw to my astounded self
A butterfly had found it's food..

..of bramble blossom, on which to settle
And there in the Medina valley's dell
So close to the famous town of Cowes
I spotted my first white admiral

It flitted up and down the ride
And soon some honeysuckle found
Upon which its eggs to lay
Then off I saw the specimen glide.

Ephemeral wings that insect had
And sighting of it bought such joy
Since then I have no specimen seen
Freinds call this lepidopterist mad!

Agapanthus

African Queen, your blue flowers fly
Like sapphire gems, thrust to the sky

Azure racemes, on stalks like globes
Drops of nectar for the bees to probe.

African queen, with white -flowered head,
Where such beauty, whose wedding bed?

Bedecked by your petals, arrayed precise
A bouquet worth the ultimate price

African Queen your lilied stems
Bear such brilliance, no-one condemns

A coronet that speaks to one and all
Agapanthus, head so tall

Vagary fom the African sveldt
Survivor, victor, our hearts melt.........
To watch your sphere of jewels blow
Amid the daisies' subliminal show!

Aostan Pasture

Aostan mountains frame the scene
Lupin's golden, that stand supreme
Cornflowers catch the travellers eye
Mirror the azure blue-streaked sky
Poppies share the open ground
Screaming, the alpine swifts abound
Nature glowing in sun-basked field
Eidelweiss searching- there I kneeled...

... in awe at the created majesty
Showing it's wonder there to me!

April in Flower

Apple blossom, first of month

Pear following, white like snow

Rose climber, yellow buds are formed

I'm awestruck by their show.

Lastly lilac, scented one arrives....

All bring the joys of spring into our lives

Arachnid

Creature of the dusk and dawn
Bears the sharpest jaws
Inky thorax seems so slim
Dark it's stalking cause

Creature clambering up the drain
Watch his hairy vest
A dampy larder stored with flies
Forms the arachnid's nest

Creature feared - it's free of harm!
Brings luck, and catches mites
Look in awe at spiralled web
How strange his appetites!

Creature famed for poisoning tales
Where does your grave-yard lie?
Silence is the spiders' spell
Mystery lingers nigh!

Bardsey Isle

Ennli is place of a thousand dreams
A small pebbled bay, and iconic lighthouse
But amazingly it's home to the shearwaters
Living under the cliff-edge, where no moonlight gleams!

This natural gem is home to grey seal
That role in the surf, and sing in the mist
They lumber around as clumsy mermaids
Those calls are haunting; those brown eyes surreal

Ennli has puffins and their pufflings galore
And fulmars and gannets - soaring aloft
Nesting on jagged cliffs, which drop to the waves
Down to the Irish sea, rough to it's core

Buried in peace after service to God
Ennli is home to a ten thousand old saints
A memorial stands for pilgrims to see
And ponder the harshness of the road they trod

Bees

Bees are God's master-piece
Insects working for man
Harvesting pollen
Making food is their plan.

Honey to sweeten, and combs to complete
Wonderous creatures into hives they retreat

Black yellow buzzers - amazing their sight
Miraculous flyers which visit the flowers
Iconic sound -our humming delight
fills Summer days -'tween   many brief showers

From buzzy bumbles to honey bee workers
All are our friends and each day never shirkers
In hives they keep clean, each new life is treasured
From springtime to harvest, bees value - unmeasured!

Bees provide honey - the sweetest of savours
Sourced from wild thyme bracts
That affects taste and flavour
To which gourmets attract

British Seaports

I've visited seaports all around these isles
The various places have sometimes raised smiles
From harbour to pier , to life-boat station
Such places have brought joy , to many a vacation.

I've visited Cromer - and fished for fresh crabs
Seen the sail lofts at Hastings- where boats store the
dabs
I once crossed the water from Southampton dock
And one day plan a trip to climb famed Plymouth Rock!

The small port of Whitby was a real delight
Its fried fish and smokeys had taste and real bite
But much further north at Fraserburgh I ate
The freshest Scottish haddock ever put on my plate!

When a very small boy with my parents in Devon
I went on a boat trip that sounded pure heaven
Tourist trips from Brixham - for mackerel the treat
In return a free dinner   - all the fish you could eat!

On my travels around our famed watery realm
I've not yet been a captain or stood on the helm
But travelling from Dover I 've waved from a ferry
Singing of White Cliffs , all my shipmates were merry.

Each port of ol' Blighty is full of past tales
And just as historical are those seaports in Wales

Like huge Pembroke Dock with its cargo and stores
Or Tenby '- with smacks, that fish off nearby shores.

Then there are giant ports like the famed Felixstowe
Where winds from the North Sea make cheeks all a-glow
It's container ships carry freight from the East
Or are importing fruit, like bananas via Geest.

Yes our ports can tell tales, like in Bristol of slaves
Who passed through from Africa.. many to their graves
Or of steam-boats with many expat soldiers on board
Returning to Tilbury after fighting abroad.

And I have worked there, seen first hand the dry dock
The iron and steel monsters a passing the lock
And for a brief while witnessed life by a river
Yes ol' Father Thames was for me a life giver.

Change ...!

Every where we see it,
in the lives of men
And in this far off country,
the time is right again.

The time is right for change, I mean
In East as well as well as West.
The people freed from Communists
Now face the Capitalist test.

Men who worked in communes
And ploughed the state owned fields
Now farm and take to market
The produce their plot yields

Gone are dreary uniforms
The choice of white or grey
Now girls can wear the latest styles
Or dress the Western way.

From the lanes are vanishing
The Slovak horse and traps
Now do men drive Ladas
To where they work perhaps?

But maybe we don't see it
The inner change I mean
Lives that are cherishing freedom
Where once much fear had been.

Cliffs of Moher

I try to recall that wonderful sight
The rocks so steep and black as night
The thrift that grew and blossomed o'er
The famous ledges of the Cliffs of Moher

Stretching up, it reached 700 feet
That coast of Clare was such a treat
With Hags Head soaring into the sky
And the climax - at O'Brians tower nearby.

Yes there I felt so amazingly small
And cried to God, the creator of all
As I felt humbled, staring down at the sea
And experienced afresh His majesty.

Devon River Outlook

I sit by the Torridge - with it's grey muddy shores
Flanked by reddish stone cottages below the green hills
The background of heathland, where jackdaws swoop
And outcrops of granite form the ancient Tors

I walk by the Taw, with it's wide promenade
Watch little boats cutting through the waves
See lights of Barnstaple twinkling in unison
Hear a redshank call, and watch gulls parade

I viewed Taw Head, where the stream arose
Midst peat and heather, with grazing ponies
Soon wide meanders funnelled that water
Into snake -like shapes, where marshmallow grows!

All that drained water soon forms Bideford Bay
Astrewn by wrecks and sunk ships of yore
The estuaries crossed by amazing bridges
But still lets seals bask, and the otters play

Doronicum

I search the natural world for gold
An aura of perfection, bliss
From muted shades after winter chill
As waking plants share harmonies

And there discover a border, bright:
With new leathery leaves- a great carpet...
Of leopards bane, with star-like flowers
No brighter gold e'er seen as yet!

Brighter than flash on goldfinch wing
Or buttercup kissed midst grassy hollow
Deeper fringed petals than dandelions
More gaudy than brimstone or clouded yellow

That doronicum flower can lift my mood
Out of the mire of a frosty March
Like tonic wine or an Easter egg
A sign of friendship or a rainbow's arch

Evan Evans -Peace in Poverty

In the blink of an eye, I've tapped on the door,
As I thought the dingy property was not used anymore
How wrong! That deep call :'It's my home - who are you?'
Made me freeze at it's entrance, which was damp right
through!

He was the potter of Derbyshire fame
Who had not a penny to his name
The derelict house with tiles on the floor
Had a sense that the owner didn't care anymore.

But there 'mongst the carnage of old Radio Times
Were moulds full of clay mugs, with unique designs
This recluse you see, wasn't strange in the mind
Just an eccentric potter -   and incredibly kind.

I was given by Evan an initialled wee pot
Only pennies exchanged - for he cared not a jot
For riches and trappings that money can buy
Then I bade my farewell and left with a sigh.

Face Values

Lord, why do I treat my neighbours badly
And judge them so unfairly?
Like a pack of cards I put them into suits
Yet you alone know the exact state of their hearts.

Lord, why do I distinguish black from white
For the Bible says all are precious in Your sight
In Heaven, the greatest shall be least of all
Poor men in front of you, stand tall

Lord why do I look up at kings and queens
And then look down at those I call 'have-beens'?
For as you walked the Earth you gave value
To servants I put behind me in the queue.

The answers to these questions lie within
We see others in purer light - upon confession of our sin.

Flint Men of Norfolk

I often have an axe to grind
Cos I'm a grumbling tyke
Yet there's a place in Norfolk shire
Where knappers noisily did strike...

...In comfort I now spend my days
A-walking in the light
But these ancestors mined ten feet below
The ground in darkest night

Grimes Graves is that special site
Where ancient men did toil
There on stone anvils -tools were made
From flints mined from the soil.

Astutely in those marly clays
They found to their delight
Conglomerate rocks - with quartzite bands
To make weapons with which to fight

So patiently flints were chiselled out
To fashion spears so fine
And put on wooden axe shafts stout
To kill the invading swine.

Friendship in Alpine Village

Friendship by a bed of flowers
Fountain showers
Coppered towers

Little children feel the spray
Jump before they're led away
Copper beech outlives their stay

Flycatchers chase gnat
People chat,
Remember that

Fountain sprinkles dewy screen
Sun shines through on crags of green
Martins skim past steep ravine

See white cascades,
Watch friendships made
Gods love displayed

Recapture faces, what an - art
those joys instilled within our heart
Refresh, refresh us while apart!

Gnarly Veg

African roots -   stunted and gnarly
Pound for a barrel, or white basin of barley ...?

What I 'm referring to the grocer knows
Little sugar snaps, and crinkly eddoes
Grated up mooli, and some Indian greens
With manioc tuber -   ugliest I've seen.

When there is hunger close at your door
Pounded up cassava - feeds the core
Of poorest farmers broken down
Appeasing famine - those roots long and brown

Now we see Yams and potatoes (sweet)
As an alternative veg - that 's really neat
We in our health have so much choice
Cos we've got wealth - do poor one's get a voice?

Go Placidly

(found in old St. Paul's church, Baltimore - dated 1692)

Go placidly amid the noise and haste & remember what
peace there may be in silence.
As far as is possible without surrender, be on good terms
with all persons.
Speak your truth quietly and clearly; and listen to
others,even the dull and ignorant;
they too have their story.

Avoid loud and aggressive persons, they are vexations to
the spirit.
If you compare yourself with others, you may become vain
and bitter; for always there will be people greater and
lesser than yourself.
Enjoy your achievements, as well as your plans.

Keep interested in your own career; however humble it is a
real possession in the changing fortunes of time. Exercise
caution in your business affairs, for the world is full of
trickery. But let this not blind you to the virtue there is; as
many persons strive for high ideals and everywhere life is
full of heroism.

Be yourself: especially do not feign affection. Neither
be cynical about love; for in the face of all aridity and
disenchantment it is perennial as the grass.
Take kindly the council of the years, gracefully

surrendering the things of youth. Nurture strength of
spirit to shield you in sudden misfortune.
But do not stress yourself with imaginings. Many fears are
born of fatigue and loneliness.
Beyond a wholesome discipline, be gentle on yourself.
You are a child of the Universe, no less than the trees and
the stars; you have a right to be here. And whether or not
it is clear to you, no doubt the Universe is unfolding as it
should.
Therefore be at peace with God, whoever you conceive
Him to be, and whatever your labors and aspirations, in the
noisy confusion of life keep peace with your soul.
With all it's sham and drudgery and broken dreams, it is
still a beautiful World. Be careful. Strive to be happy!

Gull Family Laridae

The angry herring gull that strives
To reach the heights before it flaps
Just like a dove that dips and soars
It's presence affects our very lives.

A common gull has virtuous ways
In wind and gale it circles and glides
But no tornado can ever stall
These laridae families' raucous lays.

The black-headed is a handsome gull
Yet many doubt his staring eyes
Knowing is he, and ever alert.
He struts menacingly o'er his cull

But as for graceful kittiwakes
Their slender wings the surf oft clip
With echoing call mimicking their name
This gull is first in the beauty stakes!

Hare Again

The hare is a creature of the spring
Seeks grassy banks to make it's form
It chases and outruns the storm

The hare has eyes to see at dusk
Widely scanning fresh hay stacks
For predators that may attack

The hare in May will seek a mate
Once chosen it strangely likes to box
With looks that are quite unorthodox

A creature that God planned for speed
With pace that can outrun a deer
The buzzard is his only fear

The baby hare is born to run
Scampering through a field of rape
Most leverets make a fast escape.

Heliopsis

Heliopsis, daisy bright
Capturing the August light
Airy stems hold golden charms
Proclaiming joy, like sacred psalms

Heliopsis loved by bees
Rich in food your nectaries,
Converts all that solar power
In the corona - magic flower

Heliopsis chocolate seeds
Upon which goldfinches feed
Hear their lively tinkling call
Harvesting husks, they have a ball.

Hungary Parody

Our tour was done in half a tickie
Enough time for just one pickie
Camera, Lichfield,
Here comes Hickey

Did the palace, gallery,
Saw the views, time for coffee
Danube's bridges?
Just can't stop me.

Ice creams - choice of any flavour
Tastebuds prompted us to savour
Buda - psssht
Magyar behaviour.

Yellow trams enhanced the view
Bought one gift and made that do.
Hungary
Nashledanou !

Iceland Flower Friends

Glory portrayed in the coolest hour
-with crashing water spout nearby
How delicate amid the spray
Flower bends to sun - it doesn't cower.
....

I find beside these quartzy stones
An Iceland poppy - orange toned
It's rooted in green slimey moss
Aside where turgid river foams

Resilent nature's bright display
These hardy plants where gnats abound
Are hidden from the human eye
But God can see their glorious ray.

Defined by silky anthers gold
Plenteous pollen there is held
Contrasts with the orange tones
Papaver blossom's, despite the cold.

I also some seclusion seek
Where silver locks and wrinkled brow
Can quietly assess this world
Where madness reigns, and strong rule weak.

In Awe of Kite

Enchantment
-Watch that steep aerobatic dive
Now joined by other kites (all five)

Excited
- Looking above fir -trees hear mewing call.
Iconic chisel tails enthral

Exhuberrant -
The pair exchange food; as, following,
They return to nest-sight on scimitar wing

Endearing
Kite, the Shakesperean bird of prey
Active from sunrise until eve of day

Lake Trasimena

Lake Trasimena rimmed with peace
Ancient communes oversee!

Swallows skim
In pure delight
Martins glide o'er lake-side tree

Evening brings a golden glow
Night-time anglers fish lake depths
An Umbrian gem - speaks more to me...

--- supposed this beauty came by chance?

No thought of our Maker's creative dance
Of joy, to paint the glistening blue
And reeds and fishes of silvery hue!

Lilies Demise

Consider white lilies
How soon that they fade
Petals once radiant
Now drop in the shade

Consider lost beauty -
a scent that effused
(a sweet sickly aroma
now no longer imbued)

But never forgetting
the pollen grains bright
That dazzled the bees
As they took off in flight!

Little Grebe

Dabchick, small fry
In this wide watery World
Demure in sable feathers
Ruffled and unfurled

Cuteness is the attribute
To give to these little grebes
Diving in the shallow pools
Nesting place of reeds

But those chestnut throat hues
Add a regal touch
Can the ploys of bold geese
Give joy like you to watch?

Dabchick diving into darkest stream
Beetles for to find
Wondrous those circles
Your legs now leave behind

Loire Recalled

I remember fondly the hot and sunny clime
Of when we stayed by the river Loire
Where vineyards settled across the hills
And cassis was served at the village bar

The name of our gite was Zig 'n Zag
Simply furnised - the flavour of Gaul?
Checked sashes and air conditioned rooms
With a picture of Mary on the kitchen wall.

But mostly I recall the cheap rich fare
Purveyed from the bistro right near that place
Daily specials scrawled on a blackboard
Served up each evening with smiles and grace!

Chief on that menu was onion soup
Followed by a home made beef ragout
Ended by fraise on frangipanes
Or some other berries served up in a mousse.

The best meal of all - eaten Saturday night
Was in a red wine ju- an exceptional taste
Pommes surrounding roast guinea fowl
It's tenderness ensured that meat didn't waste!

Lotus Lily – In Memorian

The Nile flower, I've heard it called
It's floating leaves grow there
But lesser streams and ponds are graced
By water lilies fair!

Serene Nile flower in various hues
Of white and pinky shades
Eclipsed by rosier charms and grace -
- found along life's Everglades.

Depicted in those 'glyphs and texts
Your flower was once divine
But now there but vain images
Oe'r which men often pine!

The lotus flower I've shared life with
It's petals silken bright
No longer floats along it's course
Since passing into night.

Dear Mum you were like that lotus flower
With beauty; a blessed cup;
No longer can I share your bower
Where-in we'd often sup

Your generous and unselfish ways
Meant you bloomed throughout the year
Looking upwards all your days

Determined, pain to bear.

I miss your sight, and gentle smile
The hug, and shared delight
I grieve o'er fading memories
Once filmed in black and white.

Together many lily types
With distinctive petals charm
Nymphaea nucifera - the lotus -
Will restore my sense of calm.

Magnolia Soul Soother

Magnolia Stellata is a- flowering
Caped in angelic white
Resplendent after Lenten showers
How awesome is that sight!

Your drooping bracts so startling
Bedeck those stems once bare
A beautiful bridal wreath it seems
A shrub at which to stare!

Magnolia Soulangea
The heralder of Spring
With royal ivory couplets made
Their dewy drinks to bring.

Your fleshy shades so prettily
Await late March's rays
With purple stripes to add finesse
And thus my eyes amaze.

Magpie

Magpie the raucous astute crow
What do you spy as you strut and bow?

Your beady eye sees beetles, black-berries
As tasty morsels - 'longside chicks and cherries
Variety of food, improves sheen of plumes
White and black wings breaking , the drear of winter 's
gloom!

Magpie chukkering-call, echoes in New Year
As you do mock battles, using beak like a spear

Your cocky spirit and pacy strutting gait
Make this a bird people either really love or hate.
But that glossy i mage, with trace of green and blue
Make each sighting of this corvid, a really special view!

March

March is the month for muscari
Magpies are beginning their nests
Mallards are hiding their new broods-
ducklings in sweet yellow vests.

March heralds winds from the Arctic
But camelia 's full of pink flowers
Horses are out of their stables
And frogspawn appears after showers

March is the season for lambing
Colours restoring to hedge
Swallows return from there travel
Reed warblers soon 'll churr from the sedge.

March winds still batter barn doors down
Hail -showers gett ing cold into bones
We're glad at the daffodil flowering
Soon it's Easter and all that means much

Micromoth

Micromoth, why are you here
Lowly creature body bare
Of markings, only tawny brown
Unlike spiders, no renown!

Micromoth is food for swifts
The only reason it exists?
Dead before a week of life
Unable to escape the strife ....

...Of living on Earth's dusty sphere
Where the moonless nights you share
With whip-poor-wills; these strange birds wait
For emergence of your bait.

Millers Lane

I'd love to walk down Millers Lane
In dear Dad's presence to chat again
As days gone by with love and awe
The themes of life we would explore

We'd talk of natures pure delight
The April bluebells - now in sight
Or contemplate the loud thrush call
Or late in Summer - the wheat standing tall

Then family woes and adversities
Would be talked over under those old trees
A burden shared was halved at least
Esteem for father's wisdom increased.

Other joys of planned vacations
Might be discussed, or the plight of nations
But hand on his shoulder   we'd chat away
As many fears dear Dad would allay.

At times we'd hear a yaffle's laugh
And then one Spring saw a cow with calf
Wild garlic scent made deep impression
And I would learn a little lesson.

Treasured memories these are still
The balmy June nights or September chill
Sight of the stars and deeper reflections

When I spoke of Christ - and the resurrection.

But all these pleasures have passed away
With fathers departing - back into the clay
Still the gift of sonship remains
And future rejoicing when united again.

Nature's Injustices?

Why would climbing Rose want Daisy's clothes
Or white Marguerite want pink Janet's
When there is already such injustice,
On this fallen planet?

Why in the range of this Earth's aviary
Does a magpie's wisdom sit aloft ?
Though he wears no Gucci, Prada, Burberry
In his glossy plumage , with great style he's doffed

The flowers and the cloven beasts
Are not all lavishing with beauty
Rafllessia and Cape Buffalo
Wear petals or skins out of duty!

But human-kind just has to differ
And often lust after another's looks.....
Or the power of a lion, the violets' hue
Even the knowledge from all nature's books.

Nutmeg

Nutmeg is my favourite spice
Grated fine on Mother's rice
Richly baked on semolina
In ol' spiced punch made by Auntie Ena

Victorians loved this kernel brown
Mace - its neighbour - had equal renown
Both were traded on the Indian shore
From Kerala to Bangalore

Nutmeg is known as a spice 'royal'
Cocktail makers, its powers enthral
In hot milk a 'force-majeure'
Little nut- what can you cure?

Nutmeg in that nursery rhyme
Reminds me of Iberian clime
Warm aromas through pine trees
Spicy wood smoke from chimneys

Chestnut, almond nuts, bow down
This one wears the highest crown
Alchemists for gold seek glory
Nutmeg's lure - an older story.

Ode to Little London

I remember the joys of Little London
The green verges, and the rain
The brook that edged the village street
And the chapel's weather vane.

This village had no Trafalgar Square
No Mall or Regents Park
Just daisies and thatched cottages
And sweet song of the skylark!

I remember the joy of Little London
And the love one I lost there
The inn that poured me two craft beers
To drown away my care.

Yet the simple joys of yokels chat
And ambling beside the stream
Far outweighed the sight of father Thames
With Embankments urbane theme.

Yes, mongst the gardens with their poppies
And the paddock with mare and foal
That Norfolk air and scenery
Brought healing to my soul.

Olive of Italy

Rich amber oil -pressed pure and clear
Rendered fit for pleasures of the soul
Drizzled over aubergines
Those flavours make the salad bowl..

..Shine with golden liquid streams
And taste of groves of Italy
Where salads under- plant our friend
A grey- green grandfather - an olive tree.

In profusion, the olive fruits grow
Ripe for harvest with caring hands
The tongue discerns the nutty flavour
Which make the hair and temples glow

For olive oil can souls anoint
To bless a needy heart with hope
But life's not like that liquid trail
Some ways are dry, and disappoint

Yet next year will bring another crop
And shade for sheep and cows to lie
Amid the fields of poppy flowers
For nature's joys can never stop

Parakeet Green

Parrot, green, from Asian shores
Alien - this city is not yours
Respect , please our native robins, tits
And others; you're the new tick on bird lists!

Keep away from nuts and seed
Emerald ones... go away I plead
Eloquence - to mimic- isn't heard
Your incessant squawking is absurd!!

Flying now like squadron jet
With long thin wings- unlikely pet
Your agility deserves comment
But as for your song, I justly lament !

Escapee from Victorian times
Now dozens of parikeets enjoy these climes
In Summer you thrive on such rich diet!
Then in winter time , you go real quiet .

Such foreigners may still be welcome here -
-those gaudy colours do really cheer.
With binoculars strained , I watch you perform
Because green parikeets are not the norm!

Plane Tree

Plane - you stand at 70 metres tall
(This prime example reaching 90)
Fingered branches sinewed pointing downwards
As raindrops drip from them in the Fall

Plane your girth shelters me
While traffic smuts are collected on your bark
Dappled shade makes city dwellers gather
Their favourite picnic spot, beneath this favoured tree

Plane - your Regency appeal
Lining the boulevards of our London home
Gives a real sense of your aristocracy
In Richmond or Kensington, or Stamford Hill

Plane your offspring numerous they are
Have ancestors far away from these shores
Romans saplings bought from their provinces
Remembrances of some Umbrian spa?

Plane you seem to walk along the avenues of dust
Stately but sad your inner soul
As coloured in Autumn hues
You shed fruits in October's gusts

Plane you stand lonely, at the corner of some mall
Scaly nature protects your corky rings
Insects hide beneath each palmate frond
As raucous starlings from your crown now call

Plane that accmpanies me along the road of life
How bare at times that journey seems to be
The sugar sap of promises grows too dim
But looking to the Heavens aids our strife

Provencal Herbes

Herbes de Provence I hear the cry
Smell the delicate rosemary
Essence of thyme, leaves for the stew
Cure for the ague- feverfew.

Herbes de Provence - a pinch or two
Marjoram flavours the lamb ragout
Spare the expense of savory ?
Delicate herb - make room for me!

Herbes de Provence - in Arles I hear
The locals are drinking, and let off a cheer
Aromas of herbs from the market stalls
Rise to the rooves and bounce off town walls.

Resplendent Quetzal

In the deep Guatemalan jungle
I've heard some ornithologists say
One can see a marvellous avian
Heaven-sent, clothed in fine array

The deepest red of it's wing coverts
And it's shimmering back -emerald green
Make this bird an awesome picture
Few travellers have ever seen

This is the infamous quetzal
To which Mayan Indians bowed down
The gaudy male birds with there finery
While their partners are green and light -brown

High-up in the tropical jungle
These show-off's display in the trees
Obscured as they gorge on its rich fruits
They accompany wild forest bees.

But listen all those awed by quetzals
The 'q' bird in our alphabet
While man's chopping down it's rain-forest
This gem is now under great threat !

What happens when homes for its nest sites-
The holes in the tropical trees
Can no longer be found by the quetzal
It's population will fall to it's knees!

Our God-given task of Earth stewards
Is a priviledged role with eclat
That must be passed down generations
So they'll treasure each fine habitat.

Now added to this we've a virus
That's drained us of cash for the Wild.
Let's not quieten this, our call for protection
Of all nature.. so we're reconciled!

Rest Room

I have ugly bulbous lamps above my bed
Reminds me of my past, and sick feeling
But the flower shaped shades in creamy white
Once did much in childhood healing.

I liked the bright orange paint on two of the walls
With chipped skirting from games I'd been playing
While wooden faced cupboard and bird calendars
Brought on sweet dreams as I looked at my ceiling.

Now I've new pictures on my walls
One of Venice that I purchased there
Another of the Essex countryside
Hangs silently above my bedroom chair

Returning

We hear of men and women
Who suffered much for Christ our Lord
And with a spirit of power
They died under a firy sword

We hear of youths and young men
Who walked a path of trials
But when they prayed and cried for mercy
Carried on for many more miles

Now when we are called to suffer
The heartache of those who have gone
They will act like comforting angels
Or to Scriptures on which light is shone

We look at beautiful creatures
And plants so wonderfully made
They flower with colourful petals
No human dress has displayed

Now at the promised final coming
Of Jesus, in all of his power
Those saved, will truly inherit
The glories, of Heaven's flowers

Reverend Coot

Like three score little reverends'
I spy your secret ways
In watery realm you flourish
And on small larvae graze.
No sermons postulating
How   easy your life seems
In rush and reed your nest site
You hide from faint moonbeams.

In watery realms your youngsters -
All striped with giant green feet-
make paddling   seem no effort
Why? You never show defeat!
Yes, unlike your cousin Moorhen
Your plumes are so demure
No orange red or yellow beak
But white bill that 's so pure.

I gain delight from Mrs. Coot
As Mum steers nine balls of fluff
Unlike those ducks and geese who hoot
Your silence is enough!

Riverside Musing

In England there are rivers
That bring life to the vales
Or flow down from the moorland
Via flowery green fringed dales

I've walked along the Medway
And been barging on the Trent
Then crossed the wide Welsh Dovey
Where mudflats meet the firmament

Some meander like the Severn
Or are canalised like the Lea
But one river outshines all others
It's the Suffolk Stour for me.

Through wheat fields and rough pasture
It's weedy waters drain
Over classical English vistas
And meander across the plain.

Afringed by ancient willows
And with rushes always nigh
Its home to tiny fishes
And the emerald damselfly.

The Stour has a place in history
With Dedham at its heart
There's the famous Mill at Flatford
And that Old Master, with a cart

That paints a rural idyll
Of the Stour in days of old
When its's peaceful rippling water
Drained rough pastures lined with gold

This river still runs tidal
When past Manningtree it flows
Nearby it's plied by shipping
Plus the Danish ferry goes

Be stilled by thoughts of rivers
And the purpose of their course
Each water way an entity
That's a great life giving force.

But don't forget the Jordan river
where the Master loved to swim
And baptised the needy brothers
Learn of peace - showered forth by Him

Scottish friends

I was invited to the home of friends o'er the border
But when I arrived, all was not in order
I'd bought a wee gift - wrapped it up in a parcel
To adorn my friend's room -a Scotsman's home is his castle!

Alarmed, I 'd gotten entry to tossing the caber
Then my friends challenged me to fight with a sabre!
So glad it was lunch, with a real Scottish flavour
With neeps and tatties, a wonder to savour!

But as then for haggis - it made me quite sick
So they gave me a scotch, and that did the trick.
After tea it was games like rummy and whist
And finally hide and seek in a Scotch mist!

The losers did call the weather real mean
But, rain is the reason Scotland stays evergreen!

Yes, most Scottish people are hospitable too
They welcome a stranger with 'och aye the noo'
But my friends are special - they love the Good Book
And thankfully man and wife know how to cook!

Sea Horse

This special creature
That inhabits the sea
Is swimming warm waters
From predators to flee

It's curved spiny backbone
Iconic to them
Protects from the pred ators
Of this tiny gem.

What wonders of Nature
This Earth doth contain
On land and in Ocean
Life ever shall reign.

Sherwood's Legacy

Sherwood, denizen of thieves
Still prevails with ancient trees
Chiefly ruled by spreading oaks
For centuries worn verdant cloaks

Gnarled and beautiful the oaks remain
Shading travellers from the rain
Outlaws haunted your hallowed glades
Picked wild mushrooms in Autumnal shade!

Forest that's borne a thousand gales
Still bears marks of woodmen's trails
And holes in trunks for the tawny owls
Or the ghosts of hermits in woollen cowls.

Eerie noise the wild boars make
Find muddy pools their thirst to slake
Snuffling acorns, grubs and roots
Feasting on tender robur shoots

Yaffles bore holes - in which to lay
Eggs safe from predatives - stopped up with clay
But bear a thought for Sherwood's trunks
That were once chopped down for fuel, by monks

This green jewel centred on Edwinstowe
Exists due to royals who loved hunting so
And still today the deer roam free
Feeding on shoots and leaves of oak tree.

Nature of Sherwood keeps secrets still-
The bats domain, the whip-poor-will
The spiders web, the redstarts nest
This Nottinghamshire emerald jewelled bequest

Sicily Sensations

From dappled grey shadows
'Neath ancient olive trees
To azure depths beside rocks
Or the sound of the bees

Amid the parched field of fluffy wind-clocks
Find glossy green foliage of the citrus grove
A flourishing upon the old laval rocks
Near cobbled old villages, so easy to love

All shadowed by Etna, apex in mist
Soaring above, as for Ancient Greeks
Hosting the vineyards with white grapes profuse
Fed by the streams and spring-water creeks

Making this island wondrous to the eyes
Centuries old faces that hold and allure....
There the canaries, whistle and sing
And Maritime pines can thrive by it's shore

The fishermen's nets oft red snapper bring
To dry out on beaches; they'll no longer spawn
Soon to be added to Mamma's special pan
With pesto and herbs - a taste treat is borne.

Singing and Chatting

How to break from grey anonymity-
Just join a uniformed choir
Then you may feel loved again
Like swallows twittering on a wire.

How to sing solo, in this soul-less city
Remember the humpback whale
Who sings in the depths of our oceans
Later breaching to reveal it's tail

How to chatter along to our neighbour
Like chimps as they swing in the trees
Consider all have an opinion
Neglecting there viewpoint won't please!

Sons of Adam

All sons of Adam
All sinners, few saints,
All with their burdens,
Most with complaints

Born with a purpose,
To create and fulfil,
Show acts of kindness
Yet how many will?

Each climbs a rock-face
Scarred by deep grooves
Finding their own paths
That slowly proves……..

Some startle at traumas
On some charmed sheer surface
Others welcome ' The Challenge'
To endure in Life's race.

Some conquer boldly
While timid ones feign
Unfit, and unprepared
Overcome by each sprain

Others on this challenge
With exploring minds
Reach for the jewelled niche
Some fortune to find

Brave hearted soldiers
Take the adventurous route
Looking at each challenge
With hearts resolute

Old intrepid warriors
Their gnarled fingers employ
While clambering across barriers
Focussed on summit's joy!

For some, on Adam's challenge
They may from fear be spared
But stuck on the flat path,
No muscles have bared

All Son's have supplies, to take on their journey
Cripple or athlete, the thief or attorney
But learn from the One who trudged to hill 's crest
Whatever your route , that destiny's best.

YES The summit afar off could be an invention
For all men and boys who don't pay attention
But they have not studied the great climbing book
Which tells us of Jesus, who all men once forsook....

...for fully prepared for the mountain He faced
No other Adam, could have HIS path traced.
For the pinnacle was indeed the way of the Cross
And end for a second Adam, a cruel life loss

Soul hungry

As you go through time of trial
With your spirit feeling tired and starved
What sustenance can you draw on
That is wholesome, but God's word?

The book of love refills you
When you draw on it's rich reserves
Like if a withered brown lawn of Summer
Were replaced by fresh green turves.

If we turn to David the psalmist
We find honey from the comb
Songs which speak of beauty
That dispel our fear and gloom.

The meat we find in Scripture
Is food Jesus taught we should share
Just as grace before a meal
It should be read, and surrounded by prayer

An hour soaking in his wisdom
Will satisfy every thirst
Our path may take us through drought times
With His guidance, we'll get through life's worst

Jesus has shared all our trials,
But conquered - with resurrection power
Take heed of HIS instruction
In your hungry, thirsty hour

Siberian Squill

See the joyous Siberian squill
Amongst the hellebore borders fill
A star of warmth - for Vernal days
Tiny star-shaped flowers ablaze

Purest white their centres be
Matched by blossoming almond tree
Hoar-frost hardy little gem
In darker months remember them

Can that shining azure hue
Match that found in eyes of blue
Petal held aloft proclaim
Beauty beats the Winter's shame

Tilbury Power Station

Three strong chimneys grace the skyline
While electric blue tracery,
Embroiders each power line

Those stark brickwork faces
Transfoms that pseudo pavillion
As if to hide a fourth dimension..

.. Where lurks an ugly green dragon
If such inhabits that riverside castle

Could those puffs of smoke i've seen
Be the life- breath of this creature
Or of furnace - more sanguine?

The Linnet that Preaches

Oh linnet that sings in rusty grooves
I listen to you -my cold heart moves
Now singing soft ly , called to croon
Though I sound forlorn and out of tune.

O h linnet with notes like a tinkling bell
I   puff my chest out , to chant well.
But little passerine - you call out proud
While I am fearful to sing aloud!

Oh linnet -dun brown your feathers are
But on holly top you r chief chorister.
With reddish bib and smart wing bar
I   gain great pleasure from this avian star.

Oh linnet that sings - proclaim your king
Of all, soprano 's sweetest offering!
Help me to be grateful - for ear and voice
Along life's journey - whatever my choice.

Oh linnet you sing alone on your perch
What views you have from spire of church!
I need a vision - to use my voice on life's stage
To orate from my pulpit - so the Message not cage.

In Memoriam... the Lounge

I purchased a special card today
As it's the March weekend to display
A flowery wished, 'Happy Mother's Day

It's a different lounge now you have gone
No kisses or hugs that can respond
Oh, lonely shelf with statue, clock
- which stopped a year ago..tick tock

I cry that my tulips of bright yellow
In cut glass vase, cannot say hello
Where have you gone now, please explain-
In this COVID year of incessant pain

Until a new song I can humm
I'll think about you, my lovely Mum
I'l write this card, that makes me glum!

Tulipa Magnificat

A royal parade of colours
That sing out in every shade
Glorifying cups, or goblets, frilled
Go shimmering through each glade.

Holding the darkest secret
Drops of gold liquor chilled
They sing out the 'Magnificat',
Divinely, as God willed.

Playing tunes, their glossy trumpets
Each give back a sense of Spring
'Glory in the Highest'
Yellow, orange, red notes they sing.

Perhaps the charm of parrots
Add extra words or tones
Amazing flutes of beauty
To deck embellished thrones

If only the white-lipped petals
Could really Heaven praise
Then the tulipa 'Magnificat'
Would prolong these Easter days

So when the May-time ballads
Fire-tinged or just plain charmed
Make red or pink the borders
Let our cold hearts be warmed.

Tunisian Markets

Selling snails from Sousse square
Boiled water their poor fate
I traversed an Tunisian market
Dominating - stalls of dates

Neglet de jour are in each crate
With picture of iconic tall splayed palms
These treasured sweetmeats are idolised
In many an ancient Arabic psalm.

Merchants are selling strange produce
And snacks like spiced warm falafels
Silken scarves and beaded shawls
Or colured perfumes with deep rich smells

Walk through the soukh, with its deep aromas
Many mauve cloths draped over the walls
Oranges, kumquats boxed for sale
Sold by the traders in dark grey shawls

Wild Lands

A wagtail peeps and flits away
Across the river Lilupe
The shimmer of the damsel fly
Is echoed in the sparkling sky

Whats springs of folly lie down-stream
Past banks where shoals of minnows teem?

Forget the course of sighs and tears
The floodplains stretch to fruitful years
The history of this fine place
Was once taught in the school of grace

Mezotne' college
Please confide
The secrets of this riverside

What Latvian artisans have flown
In fear from your crazed walls of stone?

Please leave untouched old window frames
In which old pupils carved their names

The pontoon bridge on which I lie
Leads me to dream and prophecy
How many Western anglers' wait
For Latvian fish to grab their bait?

Wild Lands of Iceland

Landmanalaugar- a wind-worn space
See volcanic rocks, their ridges traced
And tracked by wild goats: feral from time
When Iceland had a harsher clime

Place of solitude - cotton grass themes
Beside the gulleys - soft water streams
Steam of geysirs spiral high!
I dream of norsemen riding by.

Landmanalaugar - in isolation
Tundra mosses the vegetation
Glistensing as dew drops catch the light
On grasses, that sheep graze with delight

Stories of bravery scream through the air
Erik the Red fought Gaukur here
Old sagas echo across the plain
Where Icelandic ponies now still reign.

How deeply we inhale there, histories of yore!
With much grace in these stories of heroic war.
Maidens were chaste, had beautiful braided hair
Knights fought gallantly, and their spoils would share.

Woodpigeon Wisdom

Columba Palumba
Is your high- falluting name
But more often as a farner's pest
Your officially classed as game

You search the fields of stubble
For beetles and and spent grain
But when the sower is at work
That's when you bring much pain.

To me you are woodpigeon
Scoffing large amounts of seed
I think your fat and lazy
And encapsulate pure greed.

But then I hear you cooing
See you strutting along my lawn
With beady eye, clean feathers
You never look forlorn !

I shouldn't judge your strange behaviour
Stabbing small birds on my fence
Or when fighting rival pigeons
When the disputes get intense!

But when I see your smart white collar
I must recant my prejudiced views
Your God's created avian
Columba - live as you choose.

This bias shouldn't follow
To all people that I o'ersee
It's not my first impressions
For God loves all humanity.

He spoke of judging fairly
With mercy shown to all
He only sees the bigger picture
And if we stand or fall !

Yorkshire Magic

I walk amid the Howardian hills
Traversing by streams with old cotton mills
From Thornton Dale down to Oswald-side
Where dippers bob, and call with pride.

I look upon the Yorkshire clouds
At their fluffy plumes I laugh aloud
The Heavens with slatey streaks tower high
Towards the glowering evening sky.

I muse upon the sheep filled field
And wonder at the farmers' yield
The bales of wool will fetch a price
which fails to match his avarice.

But then I hear the shepherd's call
To trusted collie, long-side them all
What deep rapport 'tween man and beast
That brings a glow into my breast.

.